TRAVEL WRITING

Luciana Francis

Dear Chris,

Thank you for your support - I hope you will enjoy my book.

Lucian x

Published 2022 by Against the Grain Poetry Press
againstthegrainpoetrypress.wordpress.com

ISBN 978-1-9163447-9-2

Printed by 4edge Limited
4edge.co.uk

Contents

Inventory   7

So Far   8

The Sea   9

Lunar   10

Reminiscence   11

Penha   12

Seven   13

Islands   14

memory of travel   15

Diana   16

ruins   17

Mariana Trench   18

Reluctance   19

Stockholm   20

Another Wave   21

the distance   22

The Plains   23

Manhattan Skyline   24

california poppy   25

cells   26

Fable   27

Aftermath   28

Journey to Crow   29

Relics   30

self-portrait as landscape   31

Cosmos   32

Time Travel   33

Travel Writing   34

Home, Summer   35

To the one I found, and the one we made.

Inventory

My son asks if God was ever a baby.
It depends whether you believe God is a man.
        Who was the first human,
what came before the Big Bang.
How many more years until I belong.
I am tired of being a foreigner.
Look at the contrail
as it traces another arrival.
        Mummy, what's the biggest number.
    Numbers are infinite.
So far, the only answer to my question is Poetry.
And Time is just another distance.
        And why are numbers infinite.
    So that we can count stars.

So Far

I say, hold on, girl
as she reaches out for my hand.

This view gives you a taste,
this is your first way out.

Eventually you'll learn
to close your eyes to kiss, to come.

I used to dream of a blue-eyed soul
(Why are dreams always foreign?).

Someone once showed me how
love can break your heart.

Someone told me, only love
can lead us out of the tempest.

The Sea

I

A small-town square — deserted,
as if de Chirico had painted it.

The sun casts its rays, and birdsong
colours the distance.

Trees shed their green, their leaves
a mere casualty of the season.

There's something sad in seeing
so many cars going nowhere.

II

How I long for the sea, its welcoming waves —
a carrier of salt which at times can be healing.

How I long to meander through towns
and streets of my own choosing.

Wherever we are, we find ourselves *here* —
each day made into a horizon.

We must concede defeat, for now,
and retreat like a tide.

Lunar

In the evenings I'll look out for the moon, foreign like me.
Her pious gaze, surrounded by stars.

It's been a long way to here, and right now the baby is asleep.
Mother, so many memories swaddled in salt.

I heard once that God can only be found in silence.
So here I stand under the night sky as if I was about to enter the sea,
as if I could swim. I am not afraid of this darkness.

Beyond our fence,
the sight of humble rooftops as I look for the peace that eludes me at daytime,
when the light and the hours are shackled by chores.

And I find it somewhere amongst the leaves that answer promptly to the wind;
a brief respite from the distance. I can hear my own breathing,
the sound of waves crashing.

Reminiscence

Let me tell you of a dawn ripped at the seams,
of a city mostly asleep as we

finally heard you cry out
your first breath.

How your dad helped wash you clean,
not a trace of vernix or fear,

you were handed over like a blank page —
our morning exhibit.

Let me tell you how I reached out,
lower body gripped by anaesthesia,

to gently touch your face,
and to see your eyes

as new-found punctuation
at the end of a very long sentence.

Penha

We quenched our thirst with coconut water
under a bridge as tall and vague as a temple.

We prayed in empty churches,
and carried taper candles during holy processions.

We drove with the windows down
blasting Music for the Masses,

and climbed up an unfinished building
just in time for another sunset.

I wasn't allowed to cross the road alone
until I was seven.

Seven

I circle you as if patching up my past,
as if nursing my old hunger.

I've taken to cut flowers and empty corners as if
a fortress would crumble,

if I called her.
Some time ago you asked me what her name is,

that was the week when I looked for tweezers
to try and pull out a splinter from my palm.

Islands

A magpie hops along a parking lot.
At the cemetery birds perch among prayers.

A woman wears a bright yellow parka over her sari.
My father was born far away from where he's buried.

The sun shines brightly despite its foreign accent.
My son will not inherit my exile.

This is not about going back,
this is a deep pang calling out for Pangea.

Without allies we are islands —
I need your warm hands to ward off the morning frost.

memory of travel

are foreign streets always cobbled
is that the sea at the end of the pier
is it always balmy the air
were ever the stars

Diana

The walls of my parents' rented house
were stark white and bare, except
for an heirloom cuckoo clock.

My mother took pride in cleaning.
My father argued with the voice on the radio.
It wasn't long until the city sirens lured me away.

And I recall one summer, the loud
drumming coming from the back street —
I was led inside, uninvited.

Some days after school,
we would hang out by the train track
near the wooden shack where Diana lived —

the clickety-clack of the fish plates
as the train went past, and birdsong
from a cage in her backyard.

ruins

if I went back to visit
there would be no one there to greet me

there would be no floor plan
no caption along the lonely exhibits

the prevailing silence as cold
as the bloodless marble

yes I've unshackled
the fearless horses amongst your famished cattle

I am the apple that fell far from the tree
and to flee is the opposite of disappearing

on your knees on the parquet floor
you pray but you do not listen

and the sky bares a scar
in the shape of a crescent

the crest of my wave won't fit into your glass
half-empty

sad museum
I'm glad I left

Mariana Trench

Wagtails now rule the empty playground.
Spring spreads its blessings amidst endless questions.
The sun paints a perfect circle in generous isolation.
We hang on.
Seemingly fixed stars are in constant motion.
And Moon keeping mum — more people have been there
than to the deepest part of the ocean.

Reluctance

How I cherish the minutiae of sorting laundry,
The soft chain of delicates and towels.

Our muddied garden dotted with crowns,
Tireless green among ravenous starlings.

Little one, winter is the ultimate blank page.
Let me tell you about these beginnings.

I've learned my lesson. I've earned the right.
I saw the crescent moon at the helm of a full chalice.

I followed through Saturn's trodden trail
To find a torn stitch in the bright embroidery.

This is a small stance against the imminent,
For I am not ready just yet

To stop bleeding.

Stockholm

I followed you to church
where candles were lit, and prayers
were uttered, but I wouldn't dare ask.

I thought that what you gave was it —
love — as I sat on the parquet floor
to play with hand-me-down rags:

ball gowns made from cheap chiffon,
toy plastic comb through the long, long hair,
small hands care for the barefoot doll.

Another Wave

Morning comes bearing gifts,
the early air draped in dew.

A blackbird perched
on the tallest branch —

good old fir.

Suddenly, we find ourselves
at the mercy of days.

Be it a wall, the waiting, or another wave,

all we need is a touch
to bridge the distance.

the distance

we were all like satellites once —
little one, how you remind me.

after your bedtime, the moon
clings to blue like a solitaire stud,

the cool air strewn with whispered stars.
I could stay here all night, looking upwards,

on the edge of some uncharted land,
some sort of outcast purity up for grabs,

like a single lost glove temporarily freed
from its master's hand,

found by the wayside of a road, caught
amongst forget-me-nots.

The Plains

Of all the places we've been
I find you here

After missing you for years
As I nursed, as he toddled

You were in and out of the door
Like a daily breath.

When I was younger, I dreamed
Of windows overlooking the plains

Where wild horses would graze
Where no one was a slave

Rainwater gathered in my palm.
And now look at our curtains

You replenish bird feeders
Pot up fresh cuttings

The sweet scent of roses and lavender
We watch the sun set among trees

Warm breeze wrapped up in twilight.

Manhattan Skyline

A poem instead of a phone call —

on the page each word is free
to spread its own wings.

Last night I heard this song
from years ago

(It still makes me cry
when he sings:

I'll never see your face again).

Mother, how many times
must we say goodbye?

california poppy

in the shade
I fold the laundry

hungry starlings
here's a handful of halved grapes

at sunset the petals
of orange poppies

seem to evoke a candlelit choir
and birds circle   as if

putting out a fire   i wish
the wildflowers would take over

cells

strange honeycomb
oblong
soured
and a silent army
following orders
to dig the soil
and then seal each cell
without ceremony
as relatives sob
surrounded
by those wicked trees
that branch out
like flameless wicks
from here
it looks as if
they've been gagged

Fable

If there was a door, I would open it. If there was a mountain, I would climb it. But all I see is the laundry and a lonesome pile of dishes. I clean it up. I cut a daily path across the parquet floor, under the headline: *unsung pioneer braves a dense die-cast forest*. And in the distance I notice the charcoal smoke coming out of a chimney, from a little cottage painted in pastel colours — a humble hearth in the wilderness. I enter unannounced, a lot like a birth, another unravelled yarn to be followed. And this is where I shall spend the evening, my cold hands close to the fire.

Aftermath

A bird clad in black, iridescent—
the colour of longing
in your heart.

Another path paved with the glint
of discarded armours.

(You call it *chaos.* She calls it *garden.*)

For every battle won
there's a loud caw to release the burden.

The sun sets slowly,
it is time to count your blessings

as she flies across the battlefield
to see to
her broken flowers.

Journey to Crow

About a year ago we stood here,
pulling weeds and sowing seeds.

We have since learned that we must feed
the worms before we feed the flowers.

About a year ago I heard him speak
about friends who had passed away —

I recall the sun in my eyes, as if telling me
something we're never quite ready to see.

You dug a hole for a new shrub,
your father thanked us for the book.

And here comes the irrevocable green
that grows beyond the cawing of a crow.

We blow bubbles in his memory. The wind
promptly steers them

into the ether.

Relics

For my ancestors

In our hearts there are relics
that tell us of places

carved out of pride and toil.
With a view of the sea and a port

where another ship docks,
in its hold the hunger and hopes

of many.
Upon arrival they scatter

like seedlings, mapping
a constellation of dreamers —

deliverance comes
after countless departures.

self-portrait as landscape

distance is the colour/ and the taste
of the salt/ of the sea
in my mouth/ for I travel far/
into another/ and from here
I see the pier/ I walk towards/
as if on the tip of a tongue/ of a world
open wide/ and in awe
of itself

Cosmos

Swifts weave invisible threads
across the sky.

The incoming rain
will clear the air.

Beyond the clouds,
stars bare destinies like open palms.

We hold hands,
our son plays in the grass.

We have enough faith —
there is no need for prayer.

Time Travel

As a writer I can travel
Back in time

And revisit places
By way of old scars,

Retracing my steps with the past
As a map.

Dear son, in fact, for many of us
Time & distance share a one-way ticket,

A return made possible
Only through memory.

One day you might say,
O how beautiful — and how unreliable.

Travel Writing

It's afternoon, and I am barefoot.

Undeterred by the weather,
I put pen to paper:

This moment will soon be a memory.

Shopping lists on post-it notes,
Crumpled up receipts, stapled homework,
A fortress made of building blocks.

Every morning he asks when it will snow
As I set my sights on the early crocus.

Christmas baubles shed their glitter,
Winter sparkles in the dust.

And a handful of needles from the pine tree,
Far from its forest,
Still indoors.

Home, Summer

I close my eyes, and it feels like home. Almost. Home as in warm weather and birdsong. Home as in fresh papaya, breeze blowing my curls. Home as in my hair is still naturally dark. Home as in sweat between our palms as we cross the road, and we must cross the road quickly. Home as in car horns and traffic. Home as in my pet dog wags its tail in the backyard. Home as in football on TV, on a Sunday. Home as in rice and beans. Home as in back from school, change into day clothes and go out again to ride a borrowed bike. Home as in no one will check whether I did my homework, or if my shoes are tight. Home as in stale bread for breakfast the week before payday. Home as in I miss my mother when she goes to work. Home as in my father's never been to Mexico. Home with no phone, so I need to find the nearest payphone to call a friend. Home as in I will stay out late. Home as in freshly polished parquet floor. My mother on her knees, scrubbing the rug with vinegar. Home as in heavy rains in summer. I was born in the summer. Home as in Carnival sometimes coincides with my birthday. Home as in my odalisque costume. Home as in how I love my red odalisque costume, hand-made by my mother. Home as in dancing in the streets in February, holding hands, and then letting go.

Acknowledgements

Most poems in this book were written between 2020-21. *The Sea, memory of travel, Mariana Trench, Another Wave, california poppy, cells, Cosmos,* and *Travel Writing* are specifically about the lockdown.

Many thanks to the editors of the magazines and publications in which earlier versions of some of these poems first appeared: *Cōnfingō Magazine, Consilience Journal, Kissing Dynamite,* and *Elements: Natural & The Supernatural,* an anthology published by Fawn Press.

Thank you to Maria Isakova Bennet (and The Writing Desk) for her initial editing suggestions in *Reminiscence* and *the distance,* and to Katharine Towers (via The Poetry Society) for her encouragement, suggestions and feedback on *Islands, memory of travel* and *california poppy,* and thank you to Rebecca Goss.

My heartfelt and deepest gratitude to Abegail Morley, Karen Dennison and Jessica Mookherjee for the incredible opportunity to have my voice printed onto the pages of a book.

To Anthony, for his unconditional love and support, and Tiago, who amazes me and inspires me daily.

Notes

Penha is a traditional and historical district on the east side of the city of São Paulo, Brazil, founded circa 1668. It's the place where I lived from birth until I moved to the UK in 1998.

cells was written in response to a photograph by Rafael Vilela from an article in The Guardian published on July 20th, 2020, about the toll of the coronavirus pandemic on local gravediggers in Vila Formosa, on the east side of the city of São Paulo, Brazil.

Music for the Masses is an album by Depeche Mode.

Manhattan Skyline is a song by A-ha.